Flavou Thought

Recipes for Fresh Thinking

Tom Evans

Tom Evans

Flavours of Thought : Recipes for Fresh Thinking

First Published in Great Britain 2010

ISBN 978-1-849-14047-8

© Copyright Tom Evans

www.flavoursofthought.com

Word map images used with permission from the Visual Thesaurus

http://www.visualthesaurus.com

To Louise, for giving me all the Space and Time in the World to taste these Thoughts.

Tasting Notes ...
... what readers are saying

"It is the deceptive power in its apparent simplicity which allows this book to be easily accessible to both beginners and time served devotees of personal development work. It is cleverly engineered and crafted to produce both light bulb moments and understanding, whether it's being read cover to cover, dipped into randomly or as an aide memoire when required. I do all three ... often!"

"It's brilliant! I love the idea of thinking about thoughts in a way that encourages my intuition, without embroiling me in my intellect."

"This book is intrinsically simple. Simple to read; simple to understand; simple to apply. Its simplicity is what makes it genius."

"This book takes personal development it to a different level. No stuffy 50 year old theories that people still hang their hats on. Refreshing, thought provoking and inspirational."

"I find it absolutely fascinating and I read parts of it every day. It inspires me and is already enabling me to make adjustments and to fine tune areas of my life that are in need."

"Oh my, you are brilliant with your wit and insight."

"Anti-perception is an intriguing concept and just on of the may gems to be found in Flavours of Thought which is a delightfully simple journey into personal development that can be used to build a much larger and more powerful framework that I believe hints at an even greater innovation which surprisingly is not often found in the personal development industry. I thoroughly recommend you read it and judge for yourself."

"Through gaining an understanding of the flavours in my thought process and applying the recipes, I am now positively dealing with being hurt and rejected and using them to remove frustration and to find my soul path."

"I have applied recipes to my business, to my writing and to the way I chose to live. I can now see that in every situation I have a glass half full mentality, where before there may have been despair."

"I am completely blown away by the concept of just 21 flavours creating zillions of recipes to enrich your life. You take our basic thought processes simplify them, map them and then suggest ways recipes to open up new thought process."

"This is one inspirational, magical and thought changing book that has the power to change your very being."

Tom Evans

CONTENTS

Tom Evans

Preprandial

"It only has to be true enough"
Bill Liao, author of Stone Soup
and founder of <u>www.weforest.com</u>

Nothing in this book is necessarily true.

In fact little of it is proven or even provable. Yet it's the kind of stuff which we sense is intrinsically real.

Indeed, the concepts in this book are intrinsic to our very own nature as this is a book about thought and about what and how we think. The aim of this book is simple; just to get people thinking about thinking.

Thinking about our thinking isn't easy. Imagine if a tyre knew it had a puncture and was able to repair itself while still travelling, at speed, down the fast lane of a highway. This would be a wonderful invention but obviously, with current technology, you need to stop to make that tyre change.

Similarly, this book is a pit stop for your thoughts; somewhere to pause and take a breather for a while to work out what you are thinking.

What is remarkable is that, by thinking about our thoughts in a whole new way, we can change our understanding and our very nature. What's more, we don't have to be prescriptive about exactly how we think about thoughts. Just thinking about them in a different way is enough to generate a new perspective.

The metaphor used here to generate this change in perspective is to look at thoughts as possessing different qualities - or flavours.

Furthermore by combining different flavours of thoughts in various combinations - or recipes - we can achieve a transformation in our thinking such that any issue can be resolved and any opportunity capitalised upon.

Remarkably, we go about our days not giving a second thought to our thoughts.

This is a bit of a shame as the way that we are thinking fundamentally affects how well our days go. This is not just about something as trivial as changing your outlook. For example, adopting either a glass half full or glass half empty mentality.

Your thoughts alter the world around you and your inner space too. It's even thought your thinking affects your health and it's certainly clear it can affect your demeanour which in turn can affect those around you.

What this book contains we all know is true in our hearts and in our guts. It might not be fully understood by mainstream science but some enlightened thinkers are researching the mechanisms behind what is going on in our brains and minds. The subject matter of this book has been to date the domain of philosophers and, to some extent, those with religious or spiritual leanings. As such, it has attracted nebulous and intangible labels such as faith, prayer or just plain old wishful thinking.

Many people who espouse this kind of thinking can often be heard saying. "Thoughts become things."

This is kind of right but misses the mark by some way. It is more accurate to say that "Thoughts are things."

They are as real as the book, or electronic reader, from which you are reading these words. They are as real as the photons of light that reflect off the markings on the book that enter your eyes, that then get converted to an image and interpreted as words in your mind.

These words started as thoughts in my head; I wrote them down as words and now they are creating thoughts in your head. In anyone's book, these thoughts are things. Like the light you are using to read them, thoughts are energy. They radiate out from our minds and get picked up by others.

Unlike electromagnetic radiation, they don't permeate in our three space and one time dimensions and they are not restricted by the speed of light. This is why their nature is not yet fully understood or appreciated. They are the stuff of higher dimensions - 5th, 7th and 9th to be precise. That said, when you work outside our normal dimensional realm, precision as we understand it takes on a different nature.

The flavours described here don't relate so much to those that we taste like sweetness, bitterness, saltiness, sourness and savouriness (or umami).

The world of thought is much more aligned to the world of sub-atomic particles and quanta, as this is the level upon and at which it operates. You cannot have a thought and think about it at the same time in the same way that you can't measure both a particle's position and momentum. That is of course only from our current space-time perspective.

The flavours we discuss here are oddly strangely analogous to the flavours ascribed by quantum physicists to exotic, fundamental particles known as quarks. Quarks are thought to be the building blocks of protons and neutrons which, in turn, are the building blocks of atoms and all matter.

The word quark was coined by James Joyce in Finnegan's Wake - *"Three quarks for Muster Mark"* - and hijacked by the physicist Murray Gell-Mann.

Gell-Mann, and others, further postulated that quarks come in a number of flavours types (or colours) called up, down, charm, strange, top and bottom.

Some plagiaristic fun can be had, as well as significant illumination, by further hijacking Gell-Mann's flavours and applying them to the weird and wonderful world of thoughts.

Our thoughts too can be segregated into flavour types, whether this is by coincidence or design. Note that I do not suggest there is anything more than a literary correlation.

Thoughts which are ethereal whispers can be associated with **Strangeness**.

The murmurings of our unconscious mind are almost **Charming** these 'strange' thoughts into existence and into our awareness.

Our conscious mind gives it all a sense of **Direction** and gives us the illusion that we are really 'driving the bus'.

Like the directions of the compass, thoughts can come and go in at least four directions. Our thoughts can uplift us or get us down.

Thoughts can come from the top of our heads or we can bottom them out. The up, down, top and bottom 'quarks of our mindfulness' can twist a thought on a sixpence and send it off in an entirely new direction.

So, in part 1 of this book, I have divided each of the types of thought into the three groups labelled Strangeness, Charm and Direction; each with seven flavours each.

In total, this gives us 21 different flavour ingredients for the recipes that follow. I am sure there are more and many other ways to divide and describe them and I encourage you to think of some more of your own.

It's a bit mind boggling but just these 21 thought flavours can be combined into an amazing 51,090,942,171,709,440,000 possible recipes.

Now that's a lot of thinking in anyone's book.

All matter has equivalent anti-matter as its counterpart. When they meet, they cancel each other out. Accordingly, for each flavour, you will find a description of its opposite, or anti-flavour, which represents the inability to taste it.

In part 11 of this book we will look at just 21 of these recipes. You will see though that although there are virtually unlimited recipes, that there is a natural cascading pattern from the world of the Strangeness through Charm and into Direction which leads to these 21 main flavour combinations.

For each of these recipes, you will find recommended **Occasions** when they can be used. In the same way you might have ice cream for breakfast or cereal for supper, feel free to use them when and where you 'think fit'.

That said, I do encourage you to experiment and make up your own flavour combinations as it must be remembered that nothing in this book is true.

Part 1: Flavours of Thought

These flavours are embedded in the very fabric of our DNA.

We are made from them and they drive everything we do. The world around us reflects them back to us too depending on what and how we are thinking.

Naturally in other languages, their semantic meaning will shift somewhat. This is what leads to amazing variety and cultural richness from living on this planet at this particular time.

In pre-history, before we got 'the word', we didn't possess this internal chatter ability. We were aware of our environment and our gut feelings but not yet of abstracts. The ego had not formed.

There are indeed many, many more flavours. In fact there are as many as there are words in the dictionary and a few more again. What is remarkable is how few ingredients we need to concoct gastronomic delights.

To help you recognise examples of each flavour, in the James Joyce tradition, I've even made up a new word - a flought. Each flavour lists some floughts to sum them up and you'll find them, and more, all over the Twittersphere if you search for them.

Each of these flavours is also complemented by its opposite - its anti-flavour. Observing when these are in operation is just an illuminating as for the flavour itself.

Note that the wisdom in these flavours is as old as the hills, if not a little older. They are reproduced here only in a fresh context.

Enjoy and savour.

Tom Evans

Strangeness: Ethereal Whispers

Flavour 1: Perception

Flavour 2: Excitation

Flavour 3: Germination

Flavour 4: Reception

Flavour 5: Collection

Flavour 6: Extension

Flavour 7: Comprehension

Ethereal Whispers

It is natural to assume that most thoughts are our own. Why wouldn't they be? There's a model of the world, however, that has been around for aeons where all thoughts, memories and wisdom, for everyone who has lived past, present or future, resides in a superconsciousness.

Jung popularised it as the Collective Unconscious. It has yet to be proven to exist but scientists like Rupert Sheldrake has postulated it operates by using something he called morphic resonance. Ervin Lazlo calls it the i-Field, Information Field or Akashic Field. It is woven into the fabric of major religions such as Hinduism and Buddhism. Others refer to it as God; others still as a place where messages can come from dear departed spirits or guides, angels and ascended masters.

It is thought it exists outside our three dimensional world, packed into higher dimensions. The existence of such a field could explain a lot like, trivially, how your dog knows you are coming home or how you knew someone was about to phone. It could also explain prescience and how you know things you could not possibly know. Hence it is attractive as a concept to both philosophers and charlatans alike.

We know when we receive one of these whispers yet they remain strangely undocumented and largely unrecognised for what they might be.

As nothing in this book is necessarily true, we can postulate that the brain is a transducer which taps into the superconsciousness. Perhaps tapping into the superconsciousness is the purpose of the 90% or so of the brain that doesn't appear to have a function - yet.

These whispers are the source of light bulb moments and precognition. They travel outside space and inside time. They come in when we are least expecting them and in less than a second.

We might be day dreaming or just letting our mind wander while driving, walking the dog or washing up the dishes. In meditation and while dreaming, we are in the ideal mode to receive them. In both states, and certainly the latter, the message may come in the form of metaphor.

Some people get these whispers as a knowing; others as a voice, a sound or a vision; and some as a taste or even a smell. Most of us ignore them or are so busy that they are just swamped by the hustle and bustle of the day. If we are lucky, we may get reminded of them.

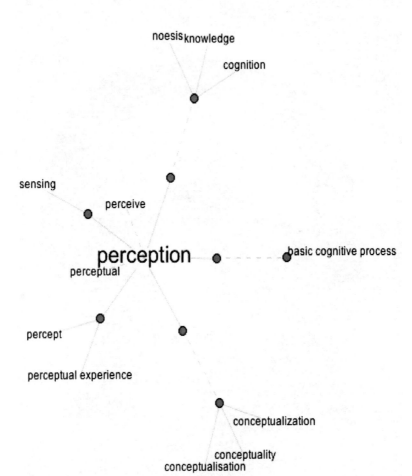

Flavour 1: Perception

We spend virtually all our days, and most of our sleeping time, completely unaware of most of what is going on around us.

This is not a bad thing, it's just the way things are and how we've evolved. Different animals notice things differently from us. For example, dogs 'see' the world as a scent map; bats and whales as a series of sound echoes.

In our modern world, more than ever, we are swamped with information. Some days you might feel completely overloaded and overwhelmed with it all. There is no time to catch a breath or to notice anything. It would be easy to conclude that our lives are a trickle of chance encounters in an ocean of missed opportunity.

How do you get off the merry-go-round and pause for breath?

The key lies in seeing the world as a set of metaphors as opposed to a given.

Fortunately we are equipped with a brain which is a fabulous pattern recognition system. It can pick out our name, or favourite football team or soap star, being spoken from the background hubbub of a party.

The devil is in the perception of the detail.

Anti-perception

Beware of falling into the trap that that the cards you have been dealt in life are all you have to play with. This is an illusion.

Don't be a busy fool; you will keep yourself from spotting the opportunities that abound.

Watch for the excuses for not following or realising your dreams.

#floughts

Perception means noticing but not acting.

Perception is about seeing the wood from the trees.

Perception is concerned with patterns.

Perception separates the lucky from the unlucky.

Perception is the initiator of change.

What does perception mean to you?

When did you last perceive something new about yourself?

Write down three new things you perceive today.

Write down three things you would like to perceive tomorrow.

irritation

innervation

excite

excitation

excitement

fervour inflammation

Flavour 2: Excitation

The result of perception is that it stirs up activity and sets transformation in motion.

The resulting excitation often exhibits itself elsewhere than our brain. We feel this particular flavour in our gut and in our 'water'. We may get shivers up and down our spine.

It is a reminder that our mind and brain are not co-sited. Our brain is the seat of consciousness and self awareness. Our mind is in every cell of our body and extends outside our physical structure.

We are still in the world of the strange here so this should not be a surprise.

The excitation can cause old beliefs and systems to crumble and disintegrate before you. What used to serve you and hold your attention is old news. This can all happen in a flash too.

The danger of this flavour of thought is that it can be uncontrollable if not used following one of the recipes herein. The baby can get thrown out with the bath water.

You can get over excited, then try and juggle too many balls and end up dropping all of them.

You can infect others too and in these cases the excitation is prone to snowball.

There is much power behind the excitation that it can be difficult to control. Like all things of power, the key here is control and moderation.

Anti-excitation

Fear of ridicule and failure stop excitation in its tracks.

Fear of the unknown and success generate avoidance tactics. The busy fool of anti-perception raises its head.

Watch for the Billy-No-Mates and the naysayers, they are drains and absorbers of your excitement.

#floughts

Excitation maybe stirred by perception.

Excitation happens in a flash.

Excitation calls for you to be a tower of strength and moderation.

Excitation is intoxicating.

What excites you?

When did you last feel excited?

What could you today to make it more exciting?

What could you engineer for your next weekend to bring new excitement into your life?

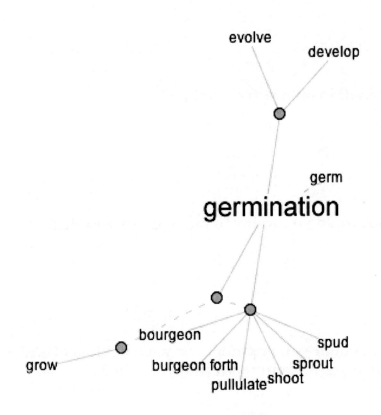

Flavour 3: Germination

The excitation forms a seed. Like all seed, it needs just the right amount loving care and attention.

Too little and it will wither and die. Too much and it will grow out of control. This flavour is all about patience and adopting a meditative approach.

There is a Zen saying, "Sitting quietly, doing nothing, spring comes, and the grass grows by itself."

In a way, this is the natural antidote to excitation. Note here that adjacent flavours complement each other.

Germination's main role is in seeding the Charming flavours in recipes as you will see later.

Germination is only successful if you are in tune with the Earth and the sky. You need a good soil to plant your seeds. At the same time, you need favourable weather conditions around you - not too much turbulence and just enough water for adequate hydration and flow.

You don't want to be too cold or too hot. You also need to be mind-full of the seasons and periodicity.

Like Goldilocks' porridge, everything must be "Just Right". Germination is dependent on the perfect marriage between earth, air, water, the Sun, the Moon and the stars.

The seeds you sow are based on all past life experience. Their life essence is formed from accumulated karma.

Anti-germination

If your initiatives are taking too much effort, you will see the fruits of your labours withering and dying.

You will experience a sense of déjà vu around repeated un-success.

Are you struggling to get something off the ground or perhaps you've lost enthusiasm.

#floughts

Germination is about having just the right conditions.

Germination relies on good timing and synchronicity.

Germination needs healthy seed stock.

Germination is a turning point in the natural rhythm of life and death.

What seeds are you nurturing right now?

What fertiliser could you use to help them grow?

How will you know when they are sprouting?

What will you do with your new crop?

Tom Evans

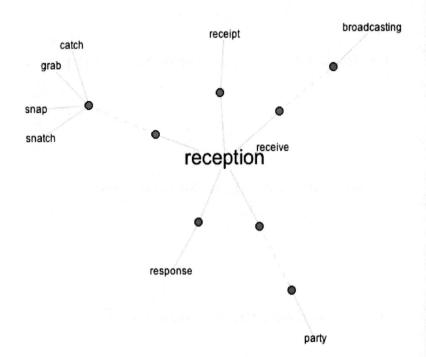

Flavour 4: Reception

Remembering that our brain is a transducer, one part of its function is to receive. The others are to interpret and comprehend and then to transmit.

Our minds are only capable, at the moment, of operating in one of these modes at a time. So if you are talking or inner-talking, you will not be able to taste the flavour of reception - it will be switched off.

In the germination flavour, you wait, you watch and you nurture. This is an ideal time to receive too.

When you dream, especially those just before you awake, your conscious mind is quiescent and you are in the ideal 'frame of mind' to receive. You just need to learn the art of remembering and interpreting the dream metaphor.

When awake, our inspirations flow in on the in breath and enter our awareness at the still point between the in and the out breath. Sometimes you also get information in via the cerebellum at the back of the head.

Just being mind-full of this is enough to switch your antennae on to external thought before you then translate and transmute it as your own.

Being receptive means reducing the barrage of incoming data and getting off the gravy train. In alchemical terms, knowledge consumed from traditional media like newspapers, TV, radio and the new social media is known as Fool's Gold.

The real riches are only available by not-thinking.

Anti-reception

Avoid transmitting constantly and those that do so.

Observe those who talk and don't listen - and yourself. Notice when your eyes are pointing downwards and your jaw is tense.

Beware and be aware of being excessively concerned about the future and reflective of the past.

#floughts

Reception requires a quiet mind.

Reception is the art of not-thinking.

Reception means you accept most thoughts are not your own.

Reception is the landing place for inspiration.

How do you receive?

What messages would you like to hear?

How would you like information to be sent to you?

How will you know if you've received them?

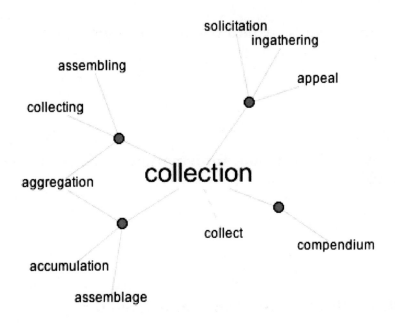

Flavour 5: Collection

Collection is the assemblage of received information prior to action.

In the same way a plant must accrue sunlight in order to photosynthesise and grow, we too must bathe in and absorb the light.

Drawing and doodling are fabulous ways to collect your thoughts. Allow your hand to be controlled by your free mind without words getting in the way.

If you are musically inclined, improvise on your instrument. It has the same effect.

Symbolically, your art will encompass the totality and more importantly bring it into the physical realm.

You will be able to fully taste the flavour and begin to see how it all fits together. You will start to spot connections between the connections that were not previously obvious. You will learn the value of possessions and the value of letting go.

As a collector, your gravitational influence will increase and just the right things will be attracted by you and drawn in by your force.

Like gravity, it is limitless in its extent and cannot be annulled by any other force.

Anti-Collection

Be aware if you find things slip from your grasp easily - money, friends, relationships.

In your jigsaw of life, count the missing pieces. Do they mean you can't appreciate the whole image yet?

Don't be afraid to horde for a while before acting.

#floughts

Collection without purpose creates a desert.

Collection creates a natural pause before concocting the most perfect recipe.

Collection is about gathering.

Collection exposes the interconnectivity.

Collections become new entities in themselves.

What collections fascinate you?

How many items do you need before you have a collection?

What is the most enjoyable aspect to collecting?

What will you do with your collections?

Flavour 6: Extension

Extension is where the fun begins.

You have collected your thoughts based on seed notions and the perception that change is about to occur.

As a Master Chef, you sense a new creation is about to unfold. You sense it is your reason to be.

Extension is all about adding value and taking common building blocks and fabricating something new. It is an excitement that stirs in your belly.

You will know it when you are doing it as it will not feel like work but fun. People will sense this in you and in what you create.

This flavour is infused with your wisdom, love and joie de vivre.

Like an extension for your house, it is wise to bring in an architect and even seek planning permission. This allows your thought to be moderated by a professional and signed off by the authorities.

This process may all add a little to the time, complexity and cost but it will pay dividends in the medium and the long term.

What you then build will last a lifetime and is capable then of being extended still further.

Anti-extension

When the walls you have already built are crumbling, you will notice the foundations you previously built on were unsound.

People will block your path and disagree with your plans.

You will feel usurped and undermined at every step.

#floughts

Extension takes what you already have and builds on it.

Extension means augmenting what exists and making it even better.

Extension allows you to reach out to places you have never been.

Extensions need careful planning.

What structures do you have in place that could benefit from being extended?

In your mind's eye, what does the new extension look and feel like?

What will you be able to do with this new space?

What steps do you need to take to extend your horizons today?

inclusion

incomprehension

comprehend

comprehension

apprehension

discernment savvy

understanding

Flavour 7: Comprehension

You know when you know something.

Something in your gut and water tells you it's true even if it runs against current thinking or your own beliefs.

You might not know why you know it or have all the detail completely mapped out - but you know it.

This different-ability we possess is sometimes referred to as claircogniscence.

This flavour is the stuff of light bulb moments. In fact, it's the spark that illuminates the filament.

It's in the strange bracket as it comes in to your head against the stream of consciousness. It feels as if it is fully formed and rounded.

It is the sum of all the first six flavours, combining them into a very savoury morsel indeed. There is still some work to be done though as it's not yet a recipe you can use in the real world and put on the menu.

It needs to percolate through the filters of our gut and heart minds. We need to analyse the what-if's, the may be's; our fears and those of our peers.

It means that we will change and we will make change happen.

It is very, very exciting.

Anti-comprehension

The opposite of knowing is sticking your head in the sand.

It's about being a victim and letting the world happen around you and to you.

It is about not asking why and being happy with the cards you have been dealt.

#floughts

Comprehension is about knowing but not knowing why you know.

Comprehension is the reason we are here.

Comprehension allows you to make step changes.

Comprehension allows you to grow exponentially.

What do you know and comprehend right now?

What don't you know and comprehend right now?

If you did know what you don't know, what difference would that make?

How would you know that you do comprehend what it is you need to know?

Tom Evans

Charm: Unconscious Murmurs

Unconscious Murmurs

A snake charmer uses his hypnotic skills to charm the coiled snake from its basket. He exercises control so that the dangerous beast is not unleashed too quickly.

From the snake's perspective, the charmer merely gives the signal for it to rise from the basket. It does not have a sense that it is being charmed or controlled. If challenged though with a stick, it will retract from where it came.

The role for the next seven flavours in the recipes that follow is to moderate and mediate the thoughts of Strangeness before we give them Direction and bring them into being.

Charming flavours operate just below our conscious awareness. They emanate from the vestigial minds of our gut and our heart and are directed through the right brain hemisphere. As such, they work holistically and, for the most time, unconsciously.

Our gut mind incidentally has the same number of neurons as a cat's brain. It is in constant communication with the billions of neurons we carry around in our head.

Although this communication is normally underneath the radar of our conscious awareness, it doesn't have to be once you tune into its signature.

We are only consciously aware of a few things each second and only one thought at a time. There are millions if not billions of signals coming from our unconscious mind each second.

Our task is to tune into the ones that matter. This is the difference between being lucky, alive, healthy and abundant - or not.

Recent magnetic image scanning shows that these types of gut- and heart-generated thoughts triggers neurological changes in our bodies 5 to 10 seconds before we are consciously aware of them.

It is they that drive the bus. They are always right although we are free to ignore and overrule them. When your gut tells you something or your heart isn't in it, it is worth paying attention to these signals.

These murmurs give rise to the illusion of Free Will.

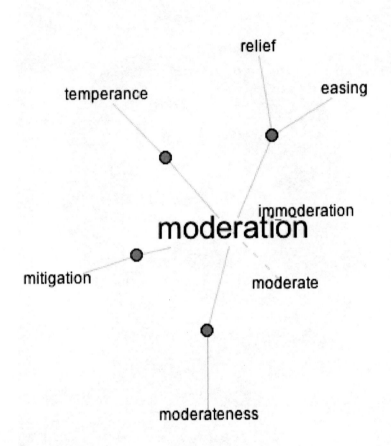

relief

easing

temperance

immoderation

moderation

mitigation

moderate

moderateness

Flavour 8: Moderation

In modern parlance and idiom, moderation has come to refer to restriction or temperance. We might moderate our drinking or moderate a debate.

It is not about limitation though. It is really about control and with this control comes great power.

Imagine that each of the thought forms that constitute the first seven flavours has the strength and ferocity of a lion. What you need is a skilled lion tamer who can control and direct that strength.

In an old style circus, the lion would be made to do tricks for entertainment and so the lion tamer could demonstrate how brave they were.

In the new energy, the enlightened 'lion tamer' allows the lion free run in protected game parks. They can hunt and breed in safety. They can be observed and studied. They are still wild animals but both under our control and our protection.

This is exactly the point of this flavour.

By observing, studying and controlling the power of the thought forms of strangeness. You can more easily charm them into existence.

Anti-moderation

The phrase "fools rush in" implies acting without moderation.

If you find yourself having to repeat work or tasks, imagine how useful that pause for breath and some '20:20 hindsight' might have been.

Watch again you don't become a busy fool.

#floughts

Moderation is about patience and control.

Moderation is about taking a pause for breath before taking action.

Moderation means not to consume more than you need.

Moderation is also about consumption of just the right things - food, knowledge, entertainment, relationships.

How are you moderating your life right now?

What would be the impact of less moderation?

What would be the impact of more moderation?

How would others know you have become more moderate?

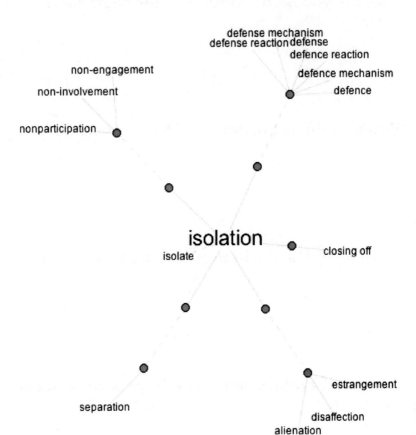

Flavour 9: Isolation

Isolation is not a position of loneliness but of strength.

Imagine the isolation you get when you are on the summit of a mountain. You can see 360 degrees all around you. You see the world in context and know your place in it.

You see the ascent route you used to get where you are and you can see the range of the next peaks you are about to conquer and master.

You have planned your route and have enough resources. You are wise and know when to rest and shelter from the elements.

In time, it even appears you are controlling the weather conditions to suit your journey. This is only because you are part of the weather not separate from it.

Isolation is not about retreating from life but concerned with fully alive powers. You will have a staff to support you and be carrying a light for others to follow.

You may be navigating new territories without a compass and find that you are creating a map for others to navigate by.

From a position of isolation, you are able to distinguish between flavours of thought.

Anti-isolation

You can be the life and soul of the party, yet, when it ends, no friends are around.

You continually seek a buzz, want the latest gadgets and can't sit still.

Happiness and contentment eludes you. It's time for that re-treat.

#floughts

Isolation is about seeing individual trees in the woods.

Isolation allows you to reap what you have sown.

Isolation gives the perfect marriage of objectivity and subjectivity.

Isolation brings the end of desolation.

Isolation is a re-treat not a retreat.

Do you feel isolated?

Do you want to be isolated?

Could you do with some isolation?

What's stopping you?

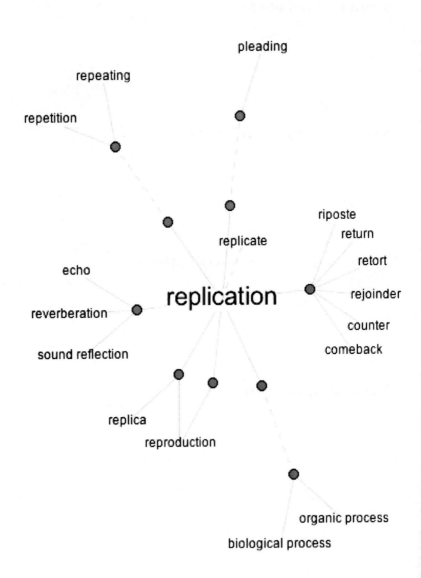

Flavour 10: Replication

Everything in nature has a natural rhythm and follows a built in pattern.

Try to reap your harvest in mid-winter, you will be too late. If you kick off a new project in spring, you will be amazed at the new energy you find within you. Spring forward, fall back.

Replication is not about going over old ground ad nauseum. It is about marching in time with nature. It is about using what is good about what pre-exists and evolving and enhancing it.

The first key is to observe the natural rhythms.

Our 'man-made' calendars obscure natural time. Electric light allows us to create our own seasons - night has become day.

Keep a daily journal; notice when you are most creative. If you are able and it is safe, allow yourself to fall asleep when you can.

Start paying attention to the phases of the Moon. From your journal, you will see your good fortune comes in cycles. You may even find it is lunar in origin. In the fullness of time, you will more easily bring in the new.

The second key is to observe what works and focus on making it even better. Spend no time worrying about problems. There is only opportunity.

Anti-Replication

If you find yourself pushing water uphill, you are out of kilter with your natural, internal seasons.

It is a karmic illusion that life is hard. Do not believe or listen to those who infer that this is so.

If you feel you are unlucky and no good fortune comes your way, try some of the recipes later that utilise this flavour. Then just watch your luck change.

#floughts

Replication is about having a perfect sense of timing.

Replication is about ebb and flow.

Replication is about reproduction with enhancement.

Replication allows what goes around to come around.

What areas of your life are working well at the moment?

What areas of your life are not so good?

What wisdom can you apply from the good areas of your life to the not so good to make them better?

Is there a pattern lurking somewhere?

counterbalance
equipoise   balance

labyrinthine sense

chemical equilibrium
sense of balance

disequilibrium
equilibrium

sense of equilibrium

vestibular sense

equilibrate

situation   state of affairs

Flavour 11: Equilibrium

A Master Chef has two main talents. They know about all the possible flavours. They also know in which perfect proportions to combine them. They have an innate sense of equilibrium

Of course, their timing is exquisite too. The diner's courses will appear just as they would like them and all in the perfect proportions

A Master Chef works with the seasons and with fresh produce. They cook hearty casseroles in mid-winter; they assemble the most delicately balanced summer salads on hot days.

Locally harvested, seasonal food arrives just when it is needed. Everything is fresh. There is no waste in this kitchen. Nobody goes home hungry; nobody is over-fed.

They are never too rushed and never too idle. Their kitchen runs like clockwork. Each member of the team knows what to do and exactly when to do it.

They wind up the coiled spring daily that drives their engine with just enough force to turn until last service.

The best chefs don't have to raise their voice; their mere presence and heightened awareness are doing all the work.

Off-balance

There is no anti-equilibrium. Anything that disturbs equilibrium will put you off balance.

Maintaining balance is as easy as riding a bike.

Explaining how to ride that bike, however, is impossible.

You will only know you are doing it properly when you are confident enough to lose the stabilisers.

#floughts

Equilibrium is about judicious combination of all the flavours.

Perfect equilibrium is easy to maintain once achieved.

Equilibrium is the perfect mix of both science and art.

Equilibrium is both the sweetest and most charming of all the flavours.

Where could you do with some more balance?

What does balance mean to you?

What is tilting the see-saw of your life?

What could you do to bring it back to level?

Tom Evans

Flavour 12: Revolution

From time to time, we have to change our thinking.

What we thought to be true turns out not to be so true after all.

Our models of the world, and the Universe, no longer fit with our observations. The world turns out to be round and not flat. Matter isn't made of solid particles but waves of probability.

What can make this worse is when both models still work. Most maps are as flat as the world they describe. Atoms exhibit both wave-like and particular behaviour.

There are two sides to each argument. Perspective dictates which is right. Old ideas and arguments have to die to give space for fresh thinking to grow.

This flavour is all about flipping your point of view and seeing the world upside down. Linguistically revolution doesn't necessarily mean change with violent struggle.

It is about re-volution and going around the circle again but this time with some changed parameters.

These changes come from a growth in experience and knowledge.

Anti-revolution

Dogma and fear are the scourge of revolution and encapsulate its antithesis.

Sticking your head in the sand will not make change go away.

All the things you most enjoy almost certainly came about from revolutionaries.

You are reading this book because Caxton's printing press made scribes redundant and allowed them to become authors in their own right.

#floughts

Revolution is healthy.

Revolution incorporates death as an essential part of life.

Revolution allows old and new models to co-exist and not to supplant each other.

Revolutionaries should be encouraged and supported.

Do you feel you are going around in circles?

How can you step off the merry-go-round?

Before you get back on, what will you change in your life?

When you get back on, how will you behave differently?

mental imagery

imaging

imagery

resource

resourcefulness

imagination imagine

imaginativeness

vision

Flavour 13: Imagination

This has to be the juiciest flavour of thought. The best imaginings are those that know no bounds and harbour no fears.

Imagination, it has been said, is the mother of invention. In-vention, like in-spiration is tied to the breath. As such, this flavour combines naturally well with others that utilise the breath.

Pure imagination uses pictures in our mind to 'image' a thought. For musicians, these can be 'pictures of sound' too. Of course, Master Chefs can imagine flavour combinations - as can tuned in consumers such as gourmands.

The best stories start with phrases like, *"Imagine a land far, far away ..."*

and, *"Just imagine ..."*

Starting a conversation using the word is enough to synchronise your audiences' thought flavour with yours.

You can use this bit of arcane magical knowledge with all the flavours and recipes incidentally.

In the new energy, the Imagineers will be the true masters of the planet and the coolest people to hang out with and to become.

Anti-imagination

Fear and self-doubt are an anathema to an Imagineer.

Life without imagination is dull as ditch water.

Imagination should never be checked but only modulated by other flavours.

#floughts

Imagination is powered by the in breath.

Imagination should be fostered - especially in the young.

Storytelling is a powerful force for the imagination.

Imagination is 24x7 - it continues while we dream.

What is blocking you from imagining?

What is limiting your imagination?

What do you imagine perfection would mean in your life?

Just imagine for a few moments what can you do today to bring that perfection in, right now.

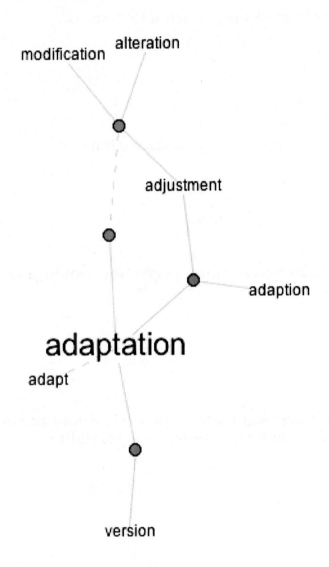

Flavour 14: Adaptation

Adaptation is woven into our DNA.

The species that innovate and adapt to their environment survive; those that remain static and intransigent can only wither and die. Only the fittest will survive.

The way to adapt is this.

Take an existing application or an idea and pause for that breath. Next observe and recognise what aspects of it represent the old patterns. Then superimpose them on a new trend and just imagine the possible spin offs.

What you have done there is to cascade the last few flavours together. The result is any number of new imaginings.

When external change occurs, adaptation is key.

You will be able to move with the times and spot new opportunities.

When you get comfortable with adaptation, new opportunities will just arrive on your doorstep as if by magic.

Anti-adaptation

If you find you are stuck in the same old rut, you will be lacking in this flavour.

Aspects of your relationships, your job and life in general will have atrophied.

You will need to adapt to stop the rot from setting in further.

#floughts

Adaptation is the application of imagination.

Adaptation is essential to survival.

Adaptation allows you to maximise your potential.

Adaptation is about low inertia.

Adaptation is the source of diversity.

What can you adapt for better purpose?

How can you adapt yourself to make things easier with others?

How can others adapt to better fit in with your plans?

What thoughts can you adapt to see these interrelationships in a new light?

Tom Evans

Direction: Who's Driving The Bus?

Flavour 15: Decision

Flavour 16: Validation

Flavour 17: Deduction

Flavour 18: Composition

Flavour 19: Connection

Flavour 20: Discrimination

Flavour 21: Cultivation

Who's Driving The Bus?

Many people go about their days either going with the flow or settling for their lot.

There is nothing wrong with that and it can even be a nice way to be. If your head doesn't rise above the parapet, you won't get spotted.

If you strive for something different in your life, however, the key lies in Directing the thoughts emanating from Strangeness and conjured up by Charm.

Like a conductor leading an orchestra, the Direction requires a degree of holistic control and engagement with both the individual musicians and the audience.

These flavours come with a caveat.

In using them, something will happen in your world as a result. So if you are going to have thoughts based on them, it is wise to make them good ones.

Einstein was quoted as saying something like, "Reality is an illusion; albeit a very persistent one."

We think our conscious mind is making decisions. Yet, as mentioned, it has been shown that there are changes in our neurology connected to actions we are about to take several seconds before we are consciously aware of them.

In which case, perhaps our conscious self-awareness is more like an observer than a director or conductor.

Our inner dialogue then is more akin to a commentary.

So to become a good director, first you must become observant. You must become comfortable with that notion that most thoughts aren't necessarily what we think of as our own.

You must learn to enjoy the ride and to take in the view before it passes you by completely.

Take a little time out to notice what you're not noticing.

From this position, true mastery becomes attainable.

resultant
termination · result
final result
outcome

decisiveness

decision

indecision

decide

conclusion
determination

Flavour 15: Decision

Once we finally make a decision, we become very focussed.

Before getting to this position, we can often be in two minds, or more, about something. This is because that is exactly what is going on. There is either an interchange going on between our left and right hemispheres or, more often, a tussle between our gut mind and our frontal lobes.

In making a decision, what is really going on is that your conscious awareness is finally in agreement with all the unconscious murmurs and ethereal whispers that have been coming your way.

We just think though that it is us that has made that decision. What is actually going on when we make a decision is that we are getting to know our own mind.

When we make a decision we are happy with, huge contentment and peace of mind usually ensues. If it doesn't you may be likely to reverse your position. This is a tell-tale sign by the way.

When you make a bad decision, you always know it at some level at the time and may regret it later. Do not be hard on yourself. Accepting without remorse that this is the way of the world and correcting your actions next time is the whole point of evolution.

Anti-decision

Beware the procrastinator as they are expert at not making a decision.

If you find yourself not knowing your own mind or not trusting your judgment, you need more of this flavour.

Use it only in a recipe combination for best results.

#floughts

Decisions are judicious execution of the will.

You intrinsically know when you make a good decision.

Decisions are like a dare from several of our unconscious murmurs.

After making a decision, it is wise to fall silent.

What decisions have you been putting off?

What would happen if you acted upon them today?

What decisions have you yet to make?

What information do you need to help you decide?

establishment

validate
validation

proof   substantiation

Flavour 16: Validation

It is wise to first validate decisions and then modify them accordingly.

You will have observed this behaviour in yourself and others. Once you decide on something, you may opt to test it out on someone.

We might state it as a fact to test the reaction, broadcasting it to all and sundry. Alternatively, we may confide in some trusted friends and advisors. Prior to seeking validation, you may like to establish the criteria that would satisfy you.

You may choose to assess what is valid and what is invalid. Ask yourself upon which basis you are making the assessment.

Either way, validation is the confirmation for the flavour of decision. It is often the choice between one course of action or the other - with inaction being an option.

Remember that the decision not to act is still a decision.

The output of validation can also be the seed for a new recipe. The same is true for all these Directive Flavours.

Anti-validation

The tale of the blind men all feeling different parts of an elephant and then comparing their observations is a great example of how not to validate.

If you ask someone of a negative disposition for their thoughts, they will see the fallibility of your plans.

An optimist might put too much of a positive spin on it.

The validation itself may require more validation.

#floughts

Validation means taking due diligence.

Validation is a healthy check and balance.

External validation allows you to sleep at night.

Internal validation strengthens the connection with your gut mind.

How do you know something is valid?

What does validity mean to you?

When does something become invalid?

Upon detecting such invalidity, what has changed? Is it the object or circumstance or your reaction to it?

synthesis

deductive reasoning

subtraction

deduct

deduce

implication

deduction

entailment

price reduction

tax deduction

discount

tax write-off

Flavour 17: Deduction

Sometimes validation is elusive. We may be operating on new ground or in new areas.

Deduction means going back to basics and working things out from first principles.

It is useful when the old model doesn't respond to validation. The decision that you are attempting to make is impossible because the data you are basing it on is flawed or incomplete.

Revolution is a fabulous flavour to combine with deduction. If something doesn't make sense, try turning it upside down to look at it from a different perspective.

For example, it is puzzling scientists where all the Dark Matter and Energy is hanging out in the Universe. Perhaps they are just looking in the wrong place with the wrong set of spectacles using completely the wrong premise.

Only by going right back to first principles and peeling off the layers of onion, can you deduce from what is really known.

Anti-deduction

The blind man who feels the elephants tusk deduces he has hold of the tooth of a large dinosaur. The blind man who holds the tail thinks he has hold of one end of a skipping rope.

When mis-information is passed on and believed as being fact, the corruption of Chinese Whispers follow.

The opposite of deduction is blind faith from which dogma emerges - or the other way around. Both science and religion are equally prone to fallibility in this regard.

#floughts

Deduction is supervisory in nature.

Deduction allows you to constitute your own view of the world.

The process of deduction sets everything in a new order.

Deduction means not taking anyone else's word for it.

What criteria do you use to make a deduction?

What process do you apply when deducing something?

How do you know when something has been deduced?

What does making that deduction mean about you?

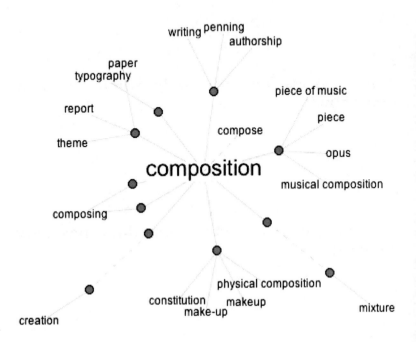

Flavour 18: Composition

Sometimes what we need does not exist and we have to make it happen.

We have an amazing ability amongst living creatures to compose new constructs from elemental sources.

What we compose though comes from an idea that starts as an ethereal whisper - either our own or that of an external agent - which is then brought to our conscious awareness as a need or opportunity.

What is so good about the flavour of composition is that it is infinite in scope and reach. Even better is our ability to judge, appreciate and savour the fruits of the composition. We know instinctively when a perfect composition has come together. It is better than the sum of its component parts.

For example, a book is a combination of words. In theory, there are a limited number of words in any language so there is a finite limit to the number of books that can be written.

Well, all you have to do is compose a single new word, like a quark or a flought, and you have just doubled the possible number of books. Note that this is a limit that we are nowhere near anyway.

The same of course is true for disciplines such as music, art and science ... and, of course, cooking!

Anti-composition

Destruction is the force that decomposes.

Decomposition that comes from death is OK as it is part of the natural rhythm and cycle.

Wanton destruction however is the antithesis of the composing force.

#floughts

Composition is about 1+1 being greater than 2.

Composition is a raison d'être.

Composition unites the disparate.

Composition is only limited by infinity.

Composition is a positive, unstoppable force.

What two components, or more, could you combine today to fabricate something entirely new?

What 'compositions' have you appreciated recently?

What feelings do you get when things come together perfectly?

What disparate elements of your life could benefit from synthesis?

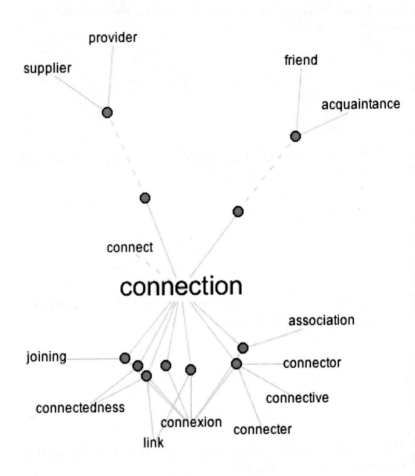

Flavour 19: Connection

Connection is a two-fold flavour.

It refers to both us understanding the connection between two or more things and fabricating a connection between them. One of course leads to the other and one may precede the other.

Art may copy Life or Life may emulate Art. It is immaterial which comes first so long as the connection is made.

Our brain works by seeing connections. It is a pattern recognition system. It learns by observing, copying and then mimicking.

When we spot a pattern we get the connection. When the pattern either repeats or appears out of sequence, we call it serendipity - assuming we're paying attention.

Listening and observing is key to making connections.

By building of the bridge between physical objects or mental constructs the connections are forged.

Master Connectors can see patterns that others fail to spot by turning the world on its head.

Anti-connection

Anti-connection is subtly different from disconnection. It is the art of not seeing patterns.

The patterns are there to make us pay attention and reconnect with our karmic path. If we don't spot the connection, it will repeat itself until we do, normally in groups of three.

If you have had three bad relationships or three unhappy jobs, ask yourself where the patterns lie.

#floughts

Connection unites and brings disparate elements together.

Connection is about spotting patterns.

Connection joins elements that were meant to be together.

All things are connected; separation is an illusion.

Where are the disconnects in your world or your thinking?

Which pairs of people could you introduce to each other today?

What state is the connection of your head and heart right now?

Say these three sentences out loud:

>**I love you my heart mind**

>**I trust you my gut mind**

>**I hear you my guiding light**

make out
pick out · distinguish
recognise · discern
spot
tell apart

indiscriminate

single out

discrimination

separate

know apart

discriminating

Flavour 20: Discrimination

If discrimination were an object, it would be like a samurai sword with an edge finely sharpened that made no sound as it swished through the air and cut right through a melon.

Discrimination is something that has to be honed; like the ability of a sommelier who instantly knows if a wine is corked from sniffing just a few molecules.

To master the art of discrimination, you have to be able to use it both externally and internally.

Externally, you must learn to notice the difference between what is important to you, what is merely metaphor and what is noise.

By doing this, the noise begins to disappear and you are only left with signals which are pertinent to you.

Internally, discrimination is all about knowing which flavour of thought you are experiencing or even commanding.

Specifically, listening and tuning into the unconscious murmurs will pay great dividends. These are what you are to pay attention to in this moment.

Anti-discrimination

If you are not art-full with your sense of discrimination, you will soon be overwhelmed with opportunity.

By tuning in to other flavours, you will stir up the universal mind-stuff and no end of new thoughts will come your way.

Choosing the good ones may take some time and involve the kissing of a few frogs before you meet your prince or princess.

#floughts

Discrimination separates the important from the non-important.

Discrimination allows us to follow our path.

External discrimination brings the signal out of the noise floor.

Internal discrimination develops your sense of 'thought smell'.

Upon which basis do you discriminate?

Do you use your head, your heart or you gut to discriminate?

How do you communicate to yourself and others that you have exercised discrimination?

What outstanding decisions require the application of discrimination right now?

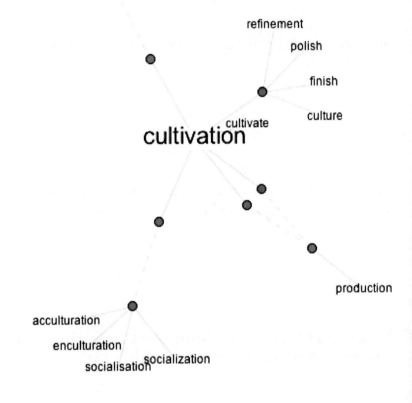

Flavour 21: Cultivation

You will have heard the phrase that it's better to give someone the ability to farm or fish than to give them the grain or fish that they think they need.

This is the essence of this last flavour. Once you know how to sense all the other flavours and then learn to combine them into recipes, you are really off and running.

You learn how to compound and consolidate from growing new opportunity from existing seeds. You become unstoppable at the same time; you have the steeds that are pulling your particular chariot well under your control.

This particular bus cannot be stopped but you are able to pick up passengers from time to time and take them to new destinations. While you travel with them, you hear their stories, learn from them and they help you keep the fuel topped up in your tank.

The road ahead seems to be mapped out for you already and you arrive at marvelous destinations without having to pay too much attention to the map.

In fact, you may find you end up drafting the map that others use to follow.

Anti-cultivation

Those without green fingers will experience poor harvests.

They will expend much effort for little return and can end up being disheartened. If this sounds like you, do not be despondent as this is just part of the lesson.

This book holds many keys and they will bear fruit in both good time and with further study.

#floughts

Cultivation makes wise use of raw materials.

Cultivation is about both reaping and sowing.

For best results, you must cultivate in tune with the seasons.

Cultivation is a mechanism for self-propelled travel.

What have you got growing in your world right now?

What would make it replicate faster?

What would make it grow stronger and healthier?

What could you change to cultivate a new way of being?

Part 11: Recipes for Fresh Thinking

This section contains a mere 21 combinations from billions of possible recipes.

As such, and as for real recipes, you can see there is a fair bit of scope for some experimentation on your part.

These particular permutations are however naturally balanced and formulated.

If you do experiment, initially, I suggest you use combinations of three flavours taking one each from the Strangeness, Charm and Direction sections.

When you get confident however, feel free to mix them with abandon.

To get more insight from these or your own recipes, refer back to the description of the flavour from Part 1.

Let me and others know via the web, email or Twitter, what you discover.

Starters:

Recipe 1: Anger at yourself

Recipe 2: Anger at someone

Recipe 3: Anger at the system

Recipe 4: Fear of the unknown

Recipe 5: Loss of confidence

Recipe 6: Fear of failure

Recipe 7: Feeling left out

These recipes deal with base emotions that stop us functioning at source. If you find yourself using these recipes, make sure you've tried the ones that apply before moving on to the mains and desserts. This will pay great dividends.

Recipe 1: Anger at yourself

Occasions

- Disappointment at your behaviour

- Embarrassment at your performance

- Annoyance at missing an opportunity

Flavours used:

Perception >> Adaptation >> Discrimination

The main aspect of this recipe is to understand that, in most cases, all anger is ultimately self-anger.

Unless you tell people, nobody else is having your feeling of anger or your particular thought. Although remember your body language may give it away for those paying enough attention.

The first step is to perceive what exactly you are angry about. It might not be the source of anger itself. It could be the result of the anger or, more likely, that you have gone and got into exactly the same position yet again. You are stuck in a rut and going round the same old loop.

If you are predisposed to blaming someone or something else, you may like to try the next recipe. If you are generally angry at yourself, read on.

Once you know what exactly you are angry about, the next flavour to apply is that of adaptation.

Think about what you can change in your approach so that the same feelings will not arise next time.

For example, a good way to perceive self anger next time is that a test has been sent your way to see if you have moved on and can handle the root cause next time around.

By adopting this strategy, in a stroke, you have applied the final flavour - that of discrimination. You have taken that samurai sword and made a clean cut between letting something anger you and observing as something that the old version of you used to get angry about.

By applying these three flavours in sequence, and in quick succession, you rise above the situation and prevent yourself getting hooked by the bait.

Recipe 2: Anger at someone

Occasions

- Being let down
- Being wronged
- Being abused

Flavours used:

Excitation >> Moderation >> Cultivation

The thoughts generated by this type of anger can easily ruin your days and keep you awake at night. Someone has hurt you and transgressed a boundary or two.

Your thoughts range from wanting some revenge or some retribution through to feeling a lack of self worth. You might just be seeking an apology.

What did you do wrong?

Why did they do that to you?

Why you ... again?

What could you have done to upset this person so much that they really upset you back worse?

You might try to be calm on the outside but inside you are silently fuming.

This recipe and flavour combination takes a lateral approach that stops this type of thought loop dead in its tracks.

First you must understand you are stuck in an excitable mode. This person's action has got you fired up.

You need a dose of moderation so you must next compose yourself to work out your strategy going forward.

Do not send that letter or fire off that email. Take stock. Was it your action that caused that person to respond in that way? If you react as you were about to, you are just playing into their hands.

It is time for you to take control using the most powerful of flavours, that of cultivation. By crafting a totally different response - which may be no response at all - you cultivate a creative force from the seeds of anger.

It may be hard to do at first but the best route forward is to send love to the person who made you angry. Love them for taking such action that allowed you to evolve and become a better person as a result.

Recipe 3: Anger at the system

Occasions

- The world seems against you

- You feel isolated

- Other people seem to have it easy

Flavours used:

Germination >> Isolation >> Decision

If you are angry at yourself or someone else, at least you can direct your rage in a certain direction. When the system is against you, it is much more difficult.

Who do you shout at?

What do you kick?

Where do you send that complaining letter?

This recipe is all about starting with a new seed stock. This seed stock, unlike the last, is resistant to dis-ease and can grow in tougher climates where others will perish. The new seed is an awareness that you are part of the system not separate from it. Any anger you have for the system is merely anger at yourself.

This awareness can be isolating as others around you will still be working with the old seeds - the idea is that it's us against the system. It is easy to slip back into the old pattern.

The key to growing this new seed is in making new choices.

By accepting that each of us creates the system from our own consciousness, you begin to control it to your benefit and to the benefit of those around you.

The temporary isolation you created to pull this off then magically attracts others who want to know your secret. You can then offer them some of your seed stock so they can grow similarly strong strains.

Once you get the confidence to show others, the system bends increasingly to your will and you see that the outcomes were your call all along.

Recipe 4: Fear of the unknown

Occasions

- Starting a new venture
- Not knowing which way to go
- Never getting projects off the ground

Flavours used:

Reception >> Replication >> Validation

This fear is enough to stop anyone in their tracks. Extreme cases can manifest as agoraphobia.

To cure this affliction, first you must be receptive to the precise conditions that bring the fear into being.

Is it all cases where things are unknown or something more specific?

If you were to have a map with which to navigate or a guide to show you the way, does the fear subside?

Once you find the key, you realise it's not the fear itself that is crippling you but the lack of an appropriate coping strategy. Once you identify where you can get the appropriate guidance from, you merely need to replicate this each time the fear comes up. Note that the strategy may change from case to case and it's healthy that it does.

The final part of this recipe is to test and validate its efficacy. You do this by assessing if the strategy has resulted in a win-win-win situation.

Has the fear subsided and do you feel you have overcome it?

Have you ended up in a better place than you were expecting?

Do you now realise that the fear wasn't real and was merely an unconscious murmur telling you there was a gap in your knowledge bank?

Recipe 5: Loss of confidence

Occasions

- Having had one too many knocks

- Picking yourself up after an illness

- Recovering from a bad review

Flavours used:

Collection >> Equilibrium >> Deduction

We all have to take knocks in our lives and it's not always easy to take them. Just telling yourself to get over it, sometimes isn't enough. If someone else says it to you at the wrong time or in the wrong place, it can even generate feeling of anger.

This feeling should not be underestimated as it's all too easy for someone to tell you not to worry about it and to pull yourself together. The fix is more subtle than this and only works when applied from within.

First you must collect both the evidence and yourself. Take some time to assess what exactly has pulled the rug from your feet. Then think back to when this has happened before. If you are able, go right back to the first occurrence.

Next you must bring in balance. This is not the balance of just offsetting a list of things you do feel confident or good about. It is about achieving a permanent state of balance such that your confidence cannot be knocked again.

This recipe needs all the flavours to be applied in parallel as opposed to in sequence. The key is in the deduction of what has unsettled you.

What does the sapping of your confidence really tell you about you?

What also does it tell you about the person or the circumstance from which the situation arose?

When you have these answers, you will learn to ask these questions first the next time it happens as opposed to taking the situation personally.

Recipe 6: Fear of failure

Occasions

- Procrastination: putting off today what you can do tomorrow

- Being a busy fool

- Always serving others first before you

Flavours used:

Extension >> Revolution >> Composition

By far the best way never to fail is not to try. Accordingly, this recipe always starts with a desire to extend yourself in some manner. The fear is only present to make you aware of possible mental or physical harm. The murmurs of your unconscious mind are your protector here.

Application of the first flavour requires you to assess how exactly you want to extend yourself. What do you want to achieve and what would be a good outcome?

Next, think about the last time you tried something similar and it ended in some kind of failure. What was the result of that failure exactly?

The worse case scenario at any time is just that you know what doesn't work. It is a mere palliative to apply that type of thinking, however.

What you must do is work out what needs to change. You need a revolution in your thinking.

Firstly realise that it is actually failure not to try. For example, there are far more authors who have written something and not published than have written and published a book. The difference between the two groups is that the latter went one extra mile.

Secondly, this time you will change your approach so that new thinking results in a different outcome.

You do this by composing both yourself and composing a new strategy. You will fail if you try exactly the same combination as last time. This time it will be different because you are thinking differently.

This recipe is subtle and, like making the perfect omelet or flipping that first pancake, do not give up on your first attempt.

Recipe 7: Feeling left out

Occasions

- Crushing loneliness

- Being a Billy-No-Mates

- Experiencing repeated patterns of failed relationships

Flavours used:

Comprehension >> Imagination >> Connection

With over six billion people on the planet, it is a good bet that there's quite a few of them that would like to be our friends.

There are bound to be others who positively want to hang out with us and some who are even candidates for perfect life long partners. Partnerships by the way can be just for friendship or business and range from liking a lot to deep love. This recipe works for them all.

The first thing to do is to fully comprehend what has caused this situation in the first place. What is it about your behaviour that causes people to shy away from you? Humans are naturally gregarious.

Then apply some imagination.

Where would the people you might like to hang out with be hanging out? With the explosion of social media sites, you can find many niche groups nowadays without leaving your home. This is very handy should Fear of the Unknown be a factor here.

Also use your imagination to think of what you might do to become more attractive.

A new hair cut or a change of wardrobe might be in order. Or why not go wild? Why not pick up a new skill or take up a new hobby? You will meet people in exactly the same boat who are also slightly outside their comfort zone and, as a result, find yourself inside yours.

The final flavour is that of connection.

This is not so much about connecting with people but making the connection of what has caused this feeling to arise in the first place.

Once you do this, it ensures it doesn't come back again.

Tom Evans

Main Courses:

Recipe 8: Being hurt

Recipe 9: Falling out of love

Recipe 10: Dealing with rejection

Recipe 11: Making a decision

Recipe 12: Handling guilt

Recipe 13: Managing grief

Recipe 14: Removing frustration

These main courses are like a lunch or an evening meal you might have at home where you just cook one hearty course. These are the recipes you can use from day to day when you want to get your life back on an even keel.

Recipe 8: Being hurt

Occasions

- Being offended
- Being ignored
- Being undervalued

Flavours used:

Perception >> Moderation >> Decision

We do not have to be physically hit to feel pain. Mental pain can carry equal if not greater weight.

The flavour of perception in this recipe requires the application of some objectivity. Ask yourself if the person or incident which caused the hurt meant to do it or not. If they did then they may only end up hurting themselves - especially if they don't have access to this recipe. If they did mean it then it's your opportunity to rise above the situation. Here's how you do it.

You must first moderate your reaction to being hurt. Do not seek revenge or look to take an eye for an eye. If appropriate let the offending party know they have hurt you. If not appropriate, the only response is to send them love and for that love to be unconditional. It should not be used to make them feel guilty about hurting you or to curry favour.

They are merely acting the part of transgressor to help you evolve. Thank them in your heart for this. By using your heart to direct the love, you will heal both parties.

Imagine a ray or beam spiraling out of the centre of your chest directed right at the heart centre of the other party. Fill it with love and empathy for the fact you both decided to experience this interaction together in order that you both can grow. Each time you breathe out, imagine it spinning faster and faster and gaining more power. This is how you generate Deep Love which is unstoppable.

Remember that the mutual evolution from these acts does not have to be co-synchronous. The other party can get the learning in their own good time and may need to act out their version of the play with others before it sinks in.

From now on, you are completely free to decide whether to be hurt or not in the future.

Recipe 9: Falling out of love

Occasions

- The end of a relationship

- The loss of spark

- Cutting cords

Flavours used:

Excitation >> Isolation >> Validation

Falling out of love is about transition and allowing cycles to come to their natural conclusion.

The excitation used in this flavour is one that you experience that you are about to move on to new pastures. Remember that the real work in any relationship starts and ends with you. This is not about replacing an old love with hate but for the love to change in its complexion and indeed its taste.

If possible you should aim to fall out of love while retaining a certain love for the other party. Note that this doesn't have to be about sexual relationships. You can love being in a company or a rock band. Love them for the time you have had together and for the times yet to come between you where your love will transcend to another level.

If possible then spend a period of isolation before falling in love again. This avoids rebounds as well as back tracking and remorse.

Use this time to fall in love with yourself but not in a narcissistic way. Give yourself 'me time' and do some things you would love to do but couldn't inside the relationship.

This will have the effect of validating your actions. You will start to see what the old relationship prevented you from doing. While seeing this objectively, it is important to keep feeding love mentally into the old relationship for helping you get to this point.

You would not now be able to appreciate 'the new' if you hadn't experienced the 'not-having' of it.

Recipe 10: Dealing with Rejection

Occasions

- Receiving criticism

- Being turned down

- When you have been told "No"

Flavours used:

Germination >> Replication >> Deduction

Rejection is a blessing. It is a sign that a path you were following is not for you. Like the last two recipes, sending love into this situation is the key.

The rejector or rejecting circumstances are doing you a huge favour. With free will of course you can resist. Or you can choose to move on and learn from it.

The seed in this case facilitates the transcending of the old thought pattern. From the rejection you are able to germinate fresh thinking. This new thinking itself takes a life of its own.

You find it is easy to replicate this approach in many other situations and indeed it can be sprinkled into other recipes to give them some piquancy.

What comes from this new approach is a method of new deduction. You begin to learn that nothing is quite as it seems. The way you used to think the world worked is not valid any more.

The veil of the illusion starts to part and you can see that your old powers of deductive reasoning were nothing compared to your new perspicacity.

You start to move into unknown territory and might combine this recipe with the one for Fear of the Unknown. This is the point even where you realise these recipes are just examples and you are completely free to make up your own concoctions.

The deduction you then make is that nothing is as it seems and everything is up for grabs and your own interpretation.

Recipe 11: Making a decision

Occasions

- When you are in two minds

- When you have too much choice

- When you reach a fork in the road

Flavours used:

Reception >> Equilibrium >> Composition

The opposite of rejection is having too much choice. Yet you will now be called to reject one of the choices. Herein lies the subtle irony between juxtaposing recipes.

To use this recipe sagely, you must remember we have free will and, at the same time, everything is preordained. You must take it on trust that both of these statements are equally true although they first appear at odds.

Reception is the first flavour to use and here the incoming message is that you will continue to experience choices until you are truly in flow. This is the output of the last recipe in this particular cook book.

You then sprinkle in some equilibrium. The use of this flavour allows either choice to be the correct one. Once chosen, the other is no longer an option, for the moment at least. The very making of a decision is the correct decision itself. Not to choose either would be a step backwards.

Next comes your master stroke. Having made either decision, you compose an outcome that simply did not occur to you before. Add some value to your chosen path and take it up a gear or three. Surprise yourself and others.

Sometimes when you do this, the route you chose not to go down suddenly reappears and you find you can have your cake and eat it after all.

All you needed to do was to make one decision and then stick to it.

Recipe 12: Handling Guilt

Occasions

• When you feel too lucky

• If you see others around you suffering

• If you have been unkind

Flavours used:

Collection >> Revolution >> Connection

Guilt can have the ability to debilitate and trip you up when things are going well. When you begin to savour the simplicity and efficacy of these recipes, life will suddenly become easier for you. People will make comment and they may even become jealous. This could stir guilt up in you.

Many belief systems teach us that life has to be hard. This is a message from false gods of man's making designed for purposes of control.

So collect your wits when guilt appears. Nobody else can breathe for you, love for you or think for you. If life is going well for you, so long as it is not at the expense of others, there is no need for guilt.

Scuba divers are taught to share their air not give it away if others are in need.

This is the revolution required in our thinking. Do not be guilty in breathing and loving your life just before others.

The final flavour seals this recipe. It is about making a big connection. Although we seem separate, we are all connected. Rather than being guilty at seemingly being better off than others, share the secret. There is more than enough to go around.

As Chief Seattle once said, "All things are connected. Whatever we do to the web of life, we do to ourselves. Whatever befalls the Earth befalls the sons and daughters of the Earth."

It is time to lose the guilt as it doesn't serve you or others.

Recipe 13: Managing Grief

Occasions

- Inconsolable loss

- Regret

- Incompletion

Flavours used:

Extension >> Imagination >> Discrimination

From time to time, often against the run of play, people, animals and things disappear from our world as they continue and play out their own karmic journey.

The issue with grief is that there is often nothing wrong with us. It's just that someone we like, respect or love decides to be no longer with us. When it happens, it really upsets our apple cart.

It would be patronising to brush this emotion away with the application of a mere three flavours of thought. Grieving is a cathartic process and it is right for it to take time and run its course.

The use of extension here refers to expanding your understanding. Life and death are a necessary part of the cycle. Nothing unreal can be preserved and nothing real can be destroyed. The soul is eternal.

Use your imagination and natural clairsentience to listen to the whispers of why people have moved on or why situations have changed. It is because it is time for an evolutionary step and the current phase of learning has come to a natural conclusion.

Having taken this leap of faith and imagination, it is time to separate the past from the future. Use your discrimination to sense what the loss means really.

The parties who have separated have only done so temporarily. If it is appropriate, your souls will cross paths again as they have done before.

If it is not appropriate, contracts have been fulfilled and the learnings have taken place.

Recipe 14: Removing Frustration

Occasions

- Pushing water uphill
- Nothing going quite right
- Being let down by people or events

Flavours used:

Comprehension >> Adaptation >> Cultivation

When you have done everything in your power and things still aren't going your way, you will be within your rights to be frustrated.

The smart people do not waste energy. They innately sense when conditions and timing are just right. This is the main component of this recipe.

What we have to comprehend is that everything has a natural timing. If you are frustrated, it is only because you are ahead of the curve and trying to move a little faster than everyone else.

The adaptation to make here is in your approach. Rather than being frustrated, be accepting that the timing is not quite perfect. If people or events are blocking you, they are merely playing out an agreed role in your life drama.

Look at the Moon. What phase is it? The perfect time to act is from Full Moon onwards. Just after a New Moon, planning is the name of the game.

What you are cultivating here is a fresh approach to using less energy to achieve even more. By merely taking right action, you will find events conspire with you not against you.

Setting the right intent is key here. At the same time, you will always be frustrated if you are harbouring the so-called negative emotions dealt with in the first seven recipes.

The secret is that there are no such things as negative emotions. They are just positive emotions pointing in the wrong direction.

Tom Evans

Desserts:

Recipe 15: Goal Setting

Recipe 16: Growth

Recipe 17: Inspiration

Recipe 18: Falling in love

Recipe 19: Finding your soul path

Recipe 20: Your evolution

Recipe 21: Getting in flow

When you dine out at a restaurant, a good dessert really finishes off a meal. They leave you satiated and with a great taste in your mouth. These recipes are all about your evolution and growth. Unlike puddings that might expand your waist line, these will only expand your horizons.

Recipe 15: Goal setting

Occasions

- Setting a new course

- Aiming at the right targets

- Choosing realistic aims

Flavours used:

Perception >> Isolation >> Deduction

There are only two reasons you don't achieve your goals.

Firstly, that you have inner doubts and secondly that you are aiming in that wrong direction.

The flavour of perception in this recipe requires a fundamental change in thinking. When you set goals, who exactly is setting them?

If you set them using your conscious mind they are unlikely to be achieved if it is at odds with your unconscious murmurs. Your gut and heart have to be as much behind them as your head.

Here's where the next flavour comes in. By isolating the various inputs from your mind centres, you will be able to filter goals so only the ones that are bound to succeed end up getting set.

So set about process of deduction in the same way a detective would solve a crime by eliminating anything that doesn't add up.

Take a goal you have set and ask your gut mind what it thinks about it. You will get a simple "Yes" or "No" back almost before you ask the question in your head.

If you get a "No", drop the goal immediately or make it bigger or smaller and ask the question again.

If you get a "Yes", ask your heart mind if it loves the idea. If "No", ask why not. If "Yes", then write the goal down by hand on paper and go with it.

In the same way, then ask your gut and heart minds what you will learn by achieving your goals. The learning is more important than the end point. When both are in harmony, you become unstoppable.

When you are able to access your various mind centres in isolation and bring them to full agreement you will be unstoppable.

Recipe 16: Growth

Occasions

- Managing change
- Taking on new challenges
- Removing old ties that bind you

Flavours used:

Excitation >> Replication >> Composition

Now the recipes start to become truly magical. They are capable of generating more than the sum of their ingredients.

In this recipe you are excited as you know change is about to happen. If the fear of the unknown raises its head, invoking and combining other recipes is a healthy option.

This excitation needs to be modulated and harnessed otherwise you can just stick in an excitable mode. It's a nice and comfortable place to be as it seems like you are active and getting somewhere. In reality however nothing will get done if you are just too excited.

Think back to the last time you were similarly excited yet the desired end result did not quite manifest itself.

Next you replicate what was good about the last time you were in this position. You don't need to re-invent the wheel; it just needs a little finessing.

To do this, simply compose yourself. Take several breaths and note that the application of composition benefits from having some idea of where you are heading.

Have you set the right goals using the previous recipe? Have you eliminated fears and removed guilt? Is anything frustrating you? You can move on without having tackled such issues but you may temporarily experience 'growing pains'.

True growth comes when you fully own, manage and apply your power without the shackles that may have previously bound you.

Recipe 17: Inspiration

Occasions

- Receiving and processing new ideas

- Generating aha moments

- Inspiring others

Flavours used:

Germination >> Equilibrium >> Connection

Inspiration is all about receiving on the in breath and giving thanks on the out breath. Once you become comfortable with this rhythm, inspiration will flow easily and without limit.

The seeds of ideas however must be nurtured or they will simply return to the superconsciousness from where they came for someone else to act upon.

This recipe can take the output from the last two recipes. It is advisable to proceed only with ideas that fit with your goals and are part of your growth path. This way you will be flowing with the water downhill and not pushing it back against gravity.

Give ideas away to others freely that you don't want to run with and there will be no shortage of others. Before you proceed with yours though, it is vital everything is perfectly poised and in balance.

The task coming from the idea should not be too difficult or too easy. It should not be too long or too short. Like a glove that fits perfectly, you should be the only person on the planet who can carry this out. It is almost like your life's work to date has been about preparing for this moment.

You then need to connect it into the mainstream. How does it fit? What are the spin offs? Where do the end users hang out? How will it change the world and your world?

An inspiration is empty without application. You are the connector between the ethereal whisper and what we experience as physical reality.

Recipe 18: Falling in love

Occasions

- Loving yourself
- Loving the work you do
- Finding your soul mate

Flavours used:

Reception >> Revolution >> Discrimination

All love starts with self love. If there are any residues of self loathing, they will taint this recipe.

Once you truly love yourself, you apply reception. It might sound obvious but reception here refers to being ready and accepting for love to come your way. Self love does not involve the ego. It is just about being comfortable in your own skin.

The revolution in our thinking is simply this. When we are truly in love, we simply act as a mirror for the love coming right at us. Receive it freely and with thanks and it will just bounce right back at where ever it is coming from.

If you give it a nudge from your heart ray it will amplify and, like a laser, when it comes back at you again, love redoubles and so on.

So by starting with self love, you will attract the perfect partner. Noting that this recipe, like the one for falling out of love, applies to all types of partnerships. Loving the work you do and the place you live are equally as important as that ideal life partner.

The final nuance to apply is that of discrimination. There is as much a difference between being in love and being in lust as there is between loving someone and merely liking them. Both have the potential to be misconstrued.

Also, when you are lovable, you will become very attractive to many and for many different reasons. Your discernment is paramount.

Recipe 19: Finding your soul path

Occasions

• Discovering your purpose

• Voiding karma

• Seeing all as lesson

Flavours used:

Collection >> Imagination >> Cultivation

It is the strangest dichotomy of our existence that our path is both predetermined yet we have complete free will. Only when you view our lives from a higher dimensional state does this become clear.

The lessons we learn on the way are just that. Hardships are to make us stronger. Good fortune is a sign we are back on path. Reflectivity gives us experience and helps us grow.

To find your true soul path, you just have to collect a few examples of when life was just perfect. What were you doing? Who were you with? Where were you? What was so good about it?

Now imagine that every day, every hour and every minute was like that. How would you feel and what would you then achieve as a result?

This is being on path. When you love the work you do, you will never work again. Retirement, as we know it, ceases to be an option as you only retire from the treadmill system of work.

To get on your soul path requires careful cultivation of the right growing conditions. The weeds will need clearing and the soil must be enriched with nutrients. A combination of de-cluttering and adoption of a meditative practice help greatly here.

It is then a simple matter of choosing the right seeds to sow and harvesting them at just the right time. You may need a few cycles of the seasons to get the combination just right and enjoying the process is part of the journey.

Recipe 20: Your evolution

Occasions

- Ascension

- Casting off old skins

- Losing what no longer serves you

Flavours used:

Extension >> Adaptation >> Decision

Evolution relies on death and rebirth. In the new energies, it is increasingly possible to reincarnate without physical demise. You can see new incarnations as software upgrades within this life time.

There is much talk about ascension at this time. Some people also bring up the spectre of Armageddon. Both are of course possible futures if you want them to be so. A more likely scenario is that they are simply metaphors. Ascension refers to elevated thinking and Armageddon to the death of old non-serving ways.

In any event, true evolution extends way beyond the shell of our own personal existence in a physical body. We need to extend our thinking to embrace all life on this planet and possibly those beyond. Of the 2000 billion tonnes of biomass on the planet, human kind weighs in at only 100 million tonnes or so. We are only part of the consciousness of the planet, by no means all of it.

That said, your individual evolution is crucial as each one of us adds to the collective thought pool and each of us is capable of changing thinking, being and doing on behalf of the whole. This can only ever start by changing yourself.

Things staying as they are is not an option. By extending ourselves we naturally adapt. The alternative is to atrophy and die.

Blind evolution however takes a very long time to produce results. This is where the final flavour comes in to complete this dish. There is no need to wait for events to happen around you. You can decide which path your evolution will take and when to take it.

Recipe 21: Getting in flow

Occasions

- Learning to trust
- Working with a whole brain and mind
- Seeing all as metaphor

Flavours used:

Comprehension >> Moderation >> Validation

Imagine if everything was as perfect as it could possibly be. Then imagine if it could be one or two notches even better. This is what it's like to be in flow.

Opportunities and openings find you at just the right time. You always have just enough food, money and resources. Although you work hard and diligently, you are not breaking into a sweat.

This recipe is best used when you have sampled all the others. It is both the *plat du jour* and the Chef's Special. You can taste it anytime but you will only appreciate how good it is as a dish when you've tasted the others.

It requires that you first comprehend what is really going on. Being comfortable about knowing you don't know everything, is itself part of a bigger knowing in itself. If you could learn everything you would have no time for being and doing.

This is where taking things in moderation comes in big time. Learning to trust your gut and follow your heart will serve you well. The two halves of our brain, the left and right, see the world completely differently. The dichotomy again is that both are correct.

When you begin to validate the holistic view of the right hemisphere with the detailed analysis of the left, you will get in flow.

Everything presented to your senses is a metaphor as nothing inside your brain looks remotely like the outside world.

Postprandial: The Obvious

As we can only have one thought at a time, it would be foolish to think you can apply all the thoughts and recipes above on the fly. The very act of thinking about them can only happen after you have had a thought.

So the two ways to use this book are in post-analysis of a thought and by pre-planning to use a recipe.

When you apply a recipe, you will end up at an obvious position that was previously obscured to you.

In time, you will apply them without having to open the book as they become ingrained in your neurology. The flavours of thought will begin to cascade into each other and superimpose on top of each other.

This is a natural occurrence and they are known as light bulb moments. The more you use the recipes in this book, the more of these moments of light you will experience.

When you experience a light bulb moment, not only will you have a great idea but it will come into your consciousness fully formulated.

What has happened is that you've experienced at least three, if not more, flavours of thought at once.

A whisper of an idea has been murmured to your conscious mind and you've instantly worked out its significance.

With major light bulb moments, where all your neurons fire at once, it is entirely possible that you are experiencing all 21 flavours at once.

What is most remarkable about this is that it almost seems to happen in less than a second - outside Time itself.

It then takes you a while to work out all the ramifications and implications. For some, like Isaac Newton with his theories of gravitation, this can even be a lifetime's work.

The light bulb moment is only obvious after you have had it. It was obscured to you before it happened yet changes your life and those of others after it has occurred.

This is why the Obvious is the Master Flavour.

About the Author: Tomography

Tom is a 21st century renaissance man - an author, poet and occasional musician who specialises in helping authors and businesses tap into their Creative Muse.

He is a student of both the esoteric and exoteric and has been called, by others, the wizard of light bulb moments, a seer and a modern day alchemist.

He blogs and tweets under the moniker of The Bookwright. The book being wrought being the karmic book inside each and every one of us.

His 30 year career in the broadcasting and Internet industries has given him considerable commercial acumen as well as a deep appreciation and understanding of advanced technologies.

He has a knack for making these both simple to understand and empowering for others.

He uses his diverse skill set to deliver both innovation and inspiration for both authors and businesses.

Using a set of simple, elegant and thought provoking techniques, Tom will breathe life into your world and help unleash the untapped creativity inside you.

Tom teaches the arts of Whole Brain and Whole Mind Thinking and how you can experience light bulb moments on demand.

When you work with Tom, your ideas will end up actually happening so you don't see someone else emulating them a while later.

If you have a particular issue or opportunity, Tom will also concoct an individual recipe for you using these and many other possible flavours.

To find out more, visit Tom's web site:

www.tomevans.co

Other Titles

Blocks

Blocks is an easy to follow guide to unlocking your true creative potential.

This practical and comprehensive book takes you on a journey of the mind to help you banish your blocks forever and tap into an abundant flow of inspiration and creativity.

This book is for anyone who writes regularly, whether professionally or for pleasure. There are six audio tracks available as MP3 files that help you get into altered states of awareness.

Published by The Publishing Academy

ISBN for print version: 978-1905430710

ASIN for Kindle version: B0036OSA86

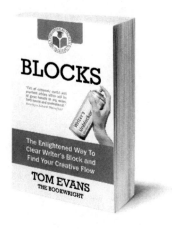

The Art and Science of Light Bulb Moments

The Art and Science of Light Bulb Moments is an interactive, educational and entertaining guide on how to have ideas on demand. This book explains how you can experience inspirations about anything, pretty much any time you like.

Light bulb moments don't have to be random.

You will learn the secrets to Whole Brain and Whole Mind Thinking, the importance of the breath and how to reconnect with your vestigial minds and the superconsciousness. Find out where ideas come from and why most thoughts aren't necessarily your own.

Reading this book will quite possibly change your world by helping you spot serendipities, making you luckier and even healthier and wealthier.

Published by O-Books - ISBN: 978-1-84694-459-8

Become a Master Chef

If you found this book engaging and intriguing, you may be thinking a couple of things like:

1. Where did all that wisdom come from?

2. What else can you do with it?

Well, I will own up to not being the generator or possessor of this wisdom. I am merely "the Translator" bringing ancient wisdom into a contemporary framework and context. What you have in this book is a précis and simulacrum of the wisdom contained in the Major Arcana of the Tarot.

Furthermore, when I wrote this book, I was aware of two things:

1. There are many more than the initial 21 flavours and I will "translate" and "publish" soon – these will come from the Minor Arcana and other arcane sources of symbology.

2. As it says in the book, there are many more than the 21 sample recipes.

Like all recipes however, there is a difference between throwing food in the microwave to warm it up and cooking a gastronomic delight worthy of a Michelin Star or three.

For this reason, I am proud to announce the launch of the Master Chef training programme.

Who is the programme for?

- Coaches, healers and therapists wanting a new toolset

- Explorers of the mind

- Parents and teachers

- Seekers of the Muse such as artists, musicians, writers, scientists

If you are interested in knowing more, email me at flavoursofthought@me.com

Tom Evans

The Cube of Karma

The Cube of Karma is a special recipe that uses all the Flavours of Thought in one big gastronomic recipe. It is delivered in a one-to-one mentoring programme.

It is an elegant technique that allows us to take stock of our journey so far and to make judgments on the course of action for our next phase of evolution.

The Cube itself is based on esoteric wisdom which is delivered in a safe and contemporary framework. It is just brimming with insight and erudition.

There is no baggage; no dogma; no need for you to change your belief set.

There is only one guarantee – after a journey around the Cube, your life will never be the same again.

For more details, see www.cubeofkarma.com

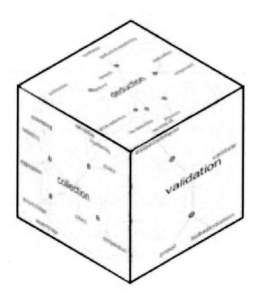

Tom Evans

Acknowledgements

No book is a solo effort.

Thanks to Bill Liao for seeding and framing my thoughts with the opening quotation.

Thanks to Sue Richardson for planting the seed that this book did not have to be very big in order to have a big impact.

Thanks to Kuumba Nia, Sally Asling and Anita-Clare Field for sampling the initial recipes and providing such detailed tasting notes.

Thanks to all my teachers, guides and mentors - past, present and future.

Thanks to Master Chef Jackie Walker for fabulous edit and attention to detail on all the speelink misteaks.

Lightning Source UK Ltd.
Milton Keynes UK
17 February 2011
167671UK00001B/47/P